BEHIND THE CAMERA

James Cameron
Ron Howard
Spike Lee
George Lucas
Rob Reiner
Steven Spielberg

George Lucas

Charles J. Shields

Chelsea House Publishers
Philadelphia

Frontis: Director George Lucas with actor Jake Lloyd on the set of *The Phantom Menace,* the first "pre-quel" in the *Star Wars* saga.

CHELSEA HOUSE PUBLISHERS

EDITOR IN CHIEF Sally Cheney
DIRECTOR OF PRODUCTION Kim Shinners
CREATIVE MANAGER Takeshi Takahashi
MANUFACTURING MANAGER Diann Grasse

STAFF FOR GEORGE LUCAS

ASSOCIATE EDITOR Ben Kim
PRODUCTION ASSISTANT Jaimie Winkler
PICTURE RESEARCHER Sarah Bloom
SERIES AND COVER DESIGNER Takeshi Takahashi
LAYOUT 21st Century Publishing and Communications, Inc.

http://www.chelseahouse.com

First Printing

1 3 5 7 9 8 6 4 2

Library of Congress Cataloging-in-Publication Data

Shields, Charles J., 1951-
  Georges Lucas / Charles J. Shields.
     p. cm. — (Behind the camera)
  ISBN 0-7910-6712-2 (hardcover)
  1. Lucas, George—Juvenile literature. 2. Motion picture producers
and directors—United States—Biography—Juvenile literature. [1.
Lucas, George. 2. Motion picture producers and directors.] I. Title.
II. Series.
  PN1998.3.L835 S54 2002
  791.43'0233'092—dc21

                    2002004387

Table of Contents

C-3PO and R2D2, the now-famous droids from the *Star Wars* movies, were just two of the strange new characters that George Lucas introduced to the world in 1977. Luckily, moviegoers embraced his vision wholeheartedly and propelled *Star Wars* to record-breaking numbers, as well as permanently etching the saga into popular culture.

Chapter **1**

Star Wars

"It's madness . . . The lines at the theaters are unbelievable."

—Spokesman for 20th Century Fox
days after the opening of *Star Wars* in 1977

TODAY, GEORGE LUCAS is known for his work on the *Star Wars* trilogy and the Indiana Jones films. His companies, Industrial Light & Magic and Skywalker Sound, count 28 Oscars to their credit. His methods of editing have revolutionized the way filmmakers work. His dinosaurs in *Jurassic Park* were the first computer-generated, living, breathing creatures with personality. And Lucas has also created educational and gaming software—titles such as *Curse of Monkey Island* and *Jedi Knight* have won awards for technical achievement and storytelling.

But on May 25, 1977 American movie audiences knew Lucas only as the young director of *American Graffiti*, a box office hit three years earlier. That film, set in California in 1962, had been a feast of nostalgia for anyone who loved custom cars, rock n' roll, and high school pranks. Were American movie audiences ready for a fantasy science-fiction adventure from him?

As thirty-three-year-old Lucas and his wife, Marcia, sat in a Los Angeles restaurant that day in May, they desperately hoped so. Eating hamburgers and watching the ticket office at Mann's Chinese Theater across the street, they hoped they hadn't gambled away their time, other people's money, and their reputations—because at Mann's that afternoon, and at only 40 other theaters nationwide, *Star Wars* was premiering.

Lucas had spent two years scripting *Star Wars*, *The Empire Strikes Back*, and *Return of the Jedi*, even though scriptwriting was not a task he enjoyed. But he knew that if *Star Wars* flopped, the two sequels would never be made. He had spent a year directing and shooting *Star Wars*, and then painstakingly cutting the footage with the assistance of his wife, a film editor.

But at 20th Century Fox, the studio that had bankrolled the picture, the buzz about *Star Wars* was not good. Warner Brothers, another major Hollywood studio, had already been burned by Lucas' first major film, *THX-1138*, in 1971. Only hardcore science-fiction buffs and highbrow critics had liked it. *Variety*, the respected newspaper of the entertainment industry, had called *THX-1138* "Abstract, handsomely stylistic but sluggish." Now the rumormongers at Fox whispered that Lucas was stubbornly making another weird, futuristic movie, instead of delivering *American Graffiti II* as they thought he should. A terrible moment came when the Lucases screened *Star Wars* for their friends, directors Steven Spielberg and Brian de Palma. When the credits ended, Spielberg and De Palma said nothing. Marcia burst into tears.

Fortunately, Fox's president, Alan Ladd, Jr. was behind the film one hundred percent. He had seen it privately and couldn't stop singing its praises. He loved it, even going so far to say that it would be historic. But among other Fox executives, there was a sense of bewilderment. Coming out of an early screening, executive producer Irwin Allen complained, "There's no stars, there's no love story, what are they clapping at?" After all, it was 1977, and Americans had not yet begun their love affair with hi-tech gadgets, eye-popping special effects in movies, and theories about black holes, alternate universes, and so on.

The United States was quite a different place then in some respects. There were only three personal computers on the market, for example—the Radio Shack TRS-80, Commodore's PET (Personal Electronics Transactor) and Steven Job's Apple computer. Jobs and his partner Steven Wozniak had just introduced their Apple II computer, the first ever with a color monitor. The basic model had 4 kilobytes of expandable RAM. Few Americans understood how a computer worked, and only a fraction of these people owned one.

On the radio, disco music was popular. Stevie Wonder had a three-week number one hit with a tribute to 1940's jazz and swing composer Duke Ellington called "Sir Duke." The top hit for the year, though, would be a gushy, sentimental song with Christian themes called "You Light Up My Life" by Debbie Boone. Elvis Presley was 42.

At the movies, character-driven films about romance and relationships were sell-outs. On the day *Stars Wars* premiered, Woody Allen's bittersweet movie *Annie Hall* opened, which later won the year's Academy Award for Best Picture. Also premiering that day, *Fun With Dick and Jane*, an offbeat spoof on the wealthy and co-starring George Segal and Jane Fonda, looked like another winner. According to a front-page article in the *New York Post*, audiences were hungrily awaiting the upcoming release of a real tearjerker—*The Other Side of Midnight*, based on a novel by best-selling author Sidney Sheldon.

To put it simply, practically no one was expecting anything on the order of Darth Vader, talking robots, leaps into hyperspace, and light sabers.

But Lucas, with Fox's help, had been preparing audiences to enter his galaxy. "It was the first film I'm aware of—and I started in the movie business in 1968—that had a complete marketing manual: research, flow charts and everything," said David Weitzner, who ran the movie's marketing as the Fox vice president for worldwide advertising. Lucas and Fox calculated that potential *Star Wars* fans were probably already Trekkies and sci-fi lovers. A special promoter was hired to drum up interest at science-fiction and comic book conventions. The studio also invited the owners of theater chains to seminars in the fall of 1976, where Fox presenters regaled them with drawings from the movie and descriptions of scenes.

Most of the guests, however—many of them middle-aged men raised on Hollywood musicals, gangster films,

Mann's Chinese Theater, whose forecourt boasts the handprints of movie icons since the 1930's, is one of the most famous Hollywood landmarks and is the scene for some of Hollywood's elite movie premieres. The legacy of Mann's Chinese Theater, where *Star Wars* was premiering, only added to George and Marcia Lucas' anxiety over the opening of their movie.

and classic stories turned into films—were a little dazed by Lucas' unique vision. "Everybody that attended was confused by words like 'R2-D2' and 'C-3PO' and 'Darth Vader,' because it was fresh and original," said Richard Einiger, who attended one of the seminars as manager of the RKO Stanley Warner Triplex in Paramus, New Jersey.

To entice mainstream audiences—whose tastes for science-fiction had largely soured because of low-budget 1950s films about flying saucers—Fox took another aggressive step. Instead of running print ads in newspapers and magazines, which wouldn't showcase the film's special effects, five commercials with action scenes had been airing regularly on television. It was a boldly going where no advertising for a movie had gone before. But would it be enough to get people shell out the money for a movie ticket in 1977—$2.75?

When it finally came time to book the movie into theaters, however, Fox chose to err on the side of caution. Normally, mainstream movies premiered at 600 or 700 theaters in the 1970s, compared with 2,500 today. *Star Wars*, on the other hand, shyly showed up on a little more than three dozen screens on May 25th.

Sitting in the restaurant, Lucas felt "tired, stressed, and thinking about nothing but all of the things I hadn't done and should have done." But it was too late. Time and money had run out. After nearly four years of work, for better or worse, *Star Wars* was going on up theater screens, finished or not, as scheduled. Now success lay in the hands of moviegoers and critics.

Out the window, however, something incredible was unfolding. As George and Marcia watched, a long line began to form in front of Mann's Chinese Theater just minutes before showtime. Rapidly, the crowd stretched down the street and around the corner. "We just fell on the floor" with amazement, Lucas remembered.

Amazement was what 14-year-old Robert Cartegna experienced in Warwick, New Jersey, too. He saw *Star Wars* three times in its first week. "We were so used to the cheesy sci-fi movies that were coming out at the time. I was completely blown away from the opening scroll to the whole space-battle scene between Leia's ship and the destroyer. There was drama. There was romance. There was everything."

The evening of the premier, a review of *Star Wars* in the *Washington Post* carried the headline, "A Spectacular Intergalactic Joyride":

George Lucas' delightful science-fiction adventure fantasy "Star Wars" . . . is a new classic in a rousing movie tradition: a space swashbuckler. Lucas, the young American filmmaker who rose to prominence with "American Graffiti" . . . has achieved a witty and exhilarating synthesis of themes and cliches from the Flash Gordon and Buck Rogers comics and serials, plus such related but less expected sources as the western, the pirate melodrama, the aerial combat melodrama and the samurai epic. . . ."Star Wars" is virtually certain of overwhelming popular and critical success. It has a real shot at approaching the phenomenal popularity of "Jaws," and I wouldn't be surprised to discover "Star Wars" in the runner-up position among modern hits before the year is out.

Even reviewers who reacted mildly to the film had to admit its appeal would draw millions of moviegoers. The reviewer for the *New York Daily News* gave *Star Wars* 3 1/2 stars out of four, but wrote, "If you are a kid at heart, a die-hard 'Star Trek' fan or just a confirmed addict of Marvel comics, 'Star Wars' will completely dazzle you."

Carrie Fisher as Princess Leia and Mark Hamill as Luke Skywalker, two characters from *Star Wars* who became icons of popular culture along with Han Solo, Chewbacca, and Darth Vader.

In its first six days, the movie grossed $2.5 million. It was the biggest hit ever in 50 years at the Mann's Chinese Theater. Managers at the other lucky theaters chosen to debut *Star Wars* added more showings. After nine days, ticket sales totaled $3.6 million, and industry watchers were calling Lucas's brainchild the sleeper of the year.

Fox's stock price nearly doubled, going from $11.75 before the movie opened to $21 by early June. By midsummer, the word was that the public was crazy for Luke Skywalker, Hans Solo, Princess Leia, and of course, Darth Vader. Some fans were arriving in costume. President Jimmy Carter told the press corps that he was jealous because his daughter had time to watch the movie in the

White House theater. By late September, grosses for the movie passed the $100 million mark.

"It's madness," a spokesman for 20th Century Fox said. "The lines at the theaters are unbelievable."

Instead of failing as a director, scriptwriter, and cinematic visionary, Lucas, according to the *Washington Post* reviewer, "has supplied 20th Century-Fox with a new lease on life."

It was the leap into hyperfame for a quiet kid from Modesto, California who said that when he was a teenager, he only went to movies to chase girls.

John Wayne was one of the most famous actors from the '50s. He appeared in many Western movies that influenced Lucas, especially about his notion of the "good guys" versus the "bad guys."

Chapter 2

The Wanderer

At their 20th [high school] reunion in 1982, Lucas' locker partner, Dennis Kamstra, remembered him as "the kind of wimp you used to slap around with a towel."

—The Associated Press

MODESTO, CALIFORNIA WAS a mid-sized town of around 60,000 when George Lucas was born there on May 14, 1944. Located in the heart of the San Joaquin Valley—a region of rich soil and pastureland—the town's economy still relies on agriculture. Every weekday, farm trucks from Modesto carrying loads of milk, cheese, almonds, apricots, melons, tomatoes, wine grapes, peaches, walnuts or poultry make their way west on Highway 99 over the coastal mountains to the markets of San Francisco, an hour and a half away. To the east are the foothills of the famed Mother Lode gold country, and much further on, the majestic Sierra Nevada Mountains and Yosemite National Park.

George Lucas, Sr. and his wife Dorothy raised their four children on a walnut ranch in Modesto, but the family business—a stationery and office supply store—provided the income for a middle-class life. "My father provided me with a lot of business principles," Lucas said, "a small-town, retail-business ethic . . . I guess I learned it." Lucas also attributes his conservative outlook on life to his dad's influence, too. But on one important subject father and son could not agree—George's future.

When George was 18, he argued heatedly with his father about it. George, Sr. wanted his namesake to take over the family business. His son absolutely refused. "I told him, 'There are two things I know for sure. One is that I will end up doing something with cars, whether I'm a racer, a mechanic . . . whatever, and two . . . I will never be president of a company.'"

Cars and machines were about the only things that held Lucas' interest for long. When his father insisted he earn his allowance by mowing the lawn, George saved up his money and purchased a riding mower—anything to have a motorized set of wheels. In a school, he was a mediocre student—actually less than mediocre at Thomas Downey High School, where he bumped along with a D+ average.

He wasn't anti-intellectual, however. It was just that school bored him. Things he could get his hands on—woodworking, art, photography, engines—absorbed him. History had the same effect. "I had a collection of history books that I was addicted to, a whole series about famous people in history from Ancient Greece and Alexander the Great, up to the Civil War—the Monitor and the Merrimac [the first ironclad battleships]." His taste in fiction ran to thrilling stories of independence and overcoming the odds—*Kidnapped* and *Treasure Island* by Robert Louis Stevenson; *Huck Finn* by Mark Twain; and *Swiss Family Robinson* by by Johann David Wyss about a shipwrecked family that uses ingenuity to construct a fortress home.

There was no television in the Lucas household until George was 10. His favorite kinds of programs were Westerns—outlaws, sheriffs, cattle-rustlers, and show-downs. Most Westerns contain at their core the seed of adventure that Lucas later used in his Star Wars films: "good guys" at a disadvantage who rely on courage, intelligence, and loyalty to overcome superior forces of "bad guys." Lucas recalls admiring actor John Wayne, whose swaggering confidence and rough but simple values made him a hero to his fans. Movie theaters didn't hold much appeal for him, however. Modesto only had one or two during his growing-up. He went now and then. Later, when he was a teenager, he said, "I only went to movies to chase girls. It took years before good movies got to my town—and foreign films? Never."

In the small town atmosphere of Modesto, a liberating moment in Lucas' life arrived when he was finally old enough to get a driver's license. Sportscar racing had seized him by then and he purchased an exotic little two-seater: a two-cylinder, four-speed Fiat Bianchina. It was so

George Lucas' primary ambition was actually to work with cars, whether it was racing them or working on them. Unfortunately, a near-fatal car accident in high school ended that dream abruptly, but ultimately led to his concept of 'The Force,' which he thought up while convalescing in the hospital after the accident.

small that it looked it belonged on a merry-go-round. Its air-cooled engine wasn't powerful enough for track racing, but the Fiat was quick enough for drag races on back roads. The body was so lightweight that the car was said to have "suicide doors."

Three days before graduating from high school, Lucas was nearly killed in an accident. Speeding toward home, he was broadsided coming around a blind corner by another student. The impact sent the Fiat careening off the road, and the car collided with tree with such force that the tree was uprooted and moved two feet, hurling Lucas through the car's open roof. At the hospital, doctors marveled that he was still alive. The police concluded that if his seatbelt hadn't mysteriously broken, he would have been restrained in the car and crushed to death. As the rest of his class graduated without him, Lucas lay in the hospital thinking "every day now is an extra day. I've been given an extra day so I've got to make the most of it."

According to those close to Lucas, it was during the weeks of rehabilitation that that he began thinking about "the Force," the energy of life often referred to in the *Star Wars* trilogy. The near-death experience moved him deeply. "The accident made me more aware of myself and my feelings. I began to trust my instincts. I had the feeling that I should go to college, and I did."

But his grades were too low to admit him right away to a four-year university. Instead, he enrolled at Modesto Junior College. It was the first time, he said, that he felt himself striving toward "realistic goals. . . . For me just setting the goals of getting decent grades in school and taking subjects I had some interest in was a big goal, and I focused on that."

Junior college presented him with a panoply of options. Which courses should he choose? He knew he enjoyed history, so he concentrated on the social sciences, taking classes in anthropology, sociology, and psychology. The larger riddle remained, however, as to what kind of occupation would use all of these subjects. He toyed with

Lucas decided to attend the University of Southern California and enroll in the cinematography program, based on his mistaken notion that it was similar to photography. Even though the two fields weren't as related as he once thought, he took to cinematography immediately and plunged headfirst into the world of filmmaking.

the idea of art school. Perhaps his interest in art and hands-on work with be a good fit with that, he thought.

Then he heard about a cinematography program at the University of Southern California in Los Angeles. Because he thought that cinematography was similar to photography, he enrolled. Lucas remembers, "And once I started in that department, I found what it was that I loved and was good at. And I realized I could do it very well, and that I enjoyed doing it. It really ignited a passion in me, and it took off from there. After that, I didn't do anything but films."

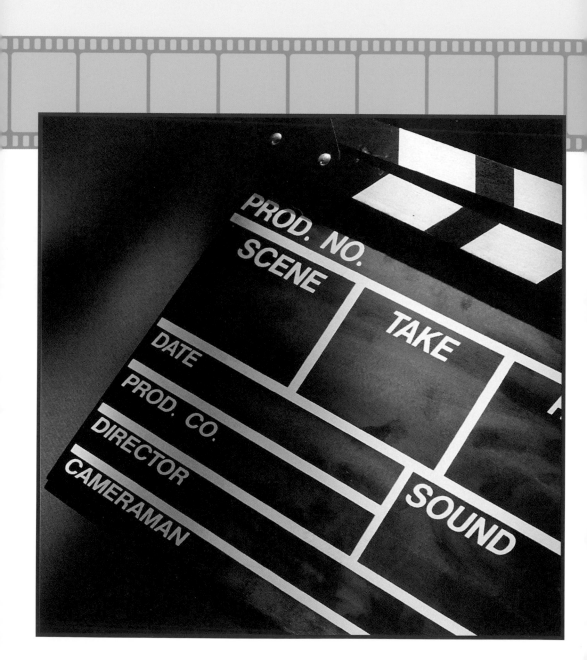

At USC, Lucas became enchanted with many aspects of the filmmaking process—especially the technical ones—and knew he had found his true passion. He even ended up working with fellow USC classmates like Steven Spielberg once out of school.

Chapter 3

Film School

"If somebody gave me a hundred feet of film, I made a movie out of it."

—George Lucas

LUCAS' GRADES WERE so much better at Modesto Junior College than in high school that he transferred easily to the University of Southern California. Soon after enrolling in junior-level classes at USC, however, he discovered that photography and cinematography were not the same, as he had mistakenly thought. But with no preconceived ideas about filmmaking, he attended classes on camerawork, editing, and lighting with an open mind.

They cast a spell on him like nothing else ever had. "Lucas found his calling at film school," wrote Dale Pollack in *Skywalking: The Life and Films of George Lucas*. "Suddenly, it was clear to him what he was going to do, and the change was dramatic . . . A lot of college students in the 1960s got high on drugs. Lucas got high on films: 'Suddenly my whole life was film—every waking hour. It was all new, neat, and exciting.'"

By a lucky stroke, he was also arriving on the filmmaking scene at the best possible time in more than a generation. Television had lured away many of Hollywood's top screenwriters and production people, forcing studios to close down or trim back by firing their youngest workers. The average age of Hollywood craftsmen when Lucas started film school was 55. There were plenty of old hands at moviemaking, in other words, but not enough newcomers coming along. If Lucas and his classmates could prove they had talent and knew how to please audiences, the filmmaking industry would welcome them with open arms. "A bit of history opened up like a seam," Lucas said, "and as many of us who could crammed in."

Like a runner vying for the lead, Lucas pulled ahead early. Many of his classmates hobbled themselves by complaining about how things not going their way: "A lot of students wandering around saying, 'Oh, I wish I could make a movie.' You know, 'I can't get in this class. I can't get any this or that,'" Lucas recalled. But Lucas had been raised in a farming community, and the formerly aimless kid had found himself at an elite school and discovered a field that enchanted him. Success was dead ahead and he went for it.

His first course was an animation class—nothing glamorous, just practical. One project involved running a mere minute of film through an animation camera and demonstrating how the camera could move up, down, left or right to help tell a story. Lucas, the technologist and machine-lover, pounced on the project with enthusiasm. A visual person by nature—someone who'd rather look at a diagram than read an explanation—he relied on pictures not dialogue to make his animation work. In his hands 32 feet of film became a movie with a beginning, middle, and end. His instructor and classmates were dazzled, as was the entire department. Lucas entered his student project in contests and won two dozen awards.

He was clearly a natural talent in filmmaking. But the 60-second animation was no fluke, either. Lucas had considerable strengths, ones that would stand him in good stead throughout his career.

First, there were his instincts about what people like to look at. He was an ordinary viewer himself, he said, and he fell back on that as an advantage. "I'm so ordinary that a lot of people can relate to me, because it's the same kind of ordinary that they are. I think it gives me insight into the mass audience. I know what I liked as a kid, and I still like it."

Then there was his "sense of structure and visual continuity," as one of his classmates at USC described it—the ability to stitch together images in a pattern that makes sense. Camera shot by camera shot, Lucas will keep his audience understanding how the story is unfolding on the screen and where they seem to be watching the action from. It could be from the perspective of appearing to stand beside a character, chasing him, or—such as in the *Star Wars* films—sitting in a cockpit dodging an oncoming hail of meteors. It's vital that audiences feel themselves carried along by a continuous flow of events, never feeling lost or confused as the filmmaker moves them around through imaginary space.

Third, Lucas learned to use two additional glues for creating a "sense of structure and visual continuity"—sound and music. He made a student film about a disc jockey called *The Emperor.* The energy of the music and the lyrics of the songs created mood and story as much as the written script. Lucas found that he could cut to different shots without losing the thread of the action because music or song lyrics formed bridges between images and characters. He would use the same technique again in *American Graffiti.* In that film, his first major commercial success, disc jockey Wolfman Jack spins records that create a continuous background to the night-time action on the streets of Modesto as kids cruise around in cars. As his career progressed, Lucas came to believe that "The sound and music are 50 percent of the entertainment in a movie." Eventually, his fascination with blending sight, sound, and music would lead to his pioneering two businesses in film technology—Industrial Light & Magic, and Skywalker Sound.

In fact, his fourth strength as a young director turned out to be his love of manipulating technology. Lucas' delight in working with technical equipment—cameras on dollies, light meters, sound boards, sets and scaffolds—provided him with a level of comfort as a director that most of his classmates didn't have. He was said to know precisely how to position cameras, set the apertures of their lens, check the lighting, and later edit the film to

Wolfman Jack was a famous radio DJ in the '50s and '60s whom Lucas employed in *American Graffiti* to spin the period songs that made up the movie's soundtrack.

get the effects he wanted. For him, the equipment of a shoot was a big toolbox he could plunge his hands into like a mechanic under the hood of a car. In fact, one of his student projects was essentially a hymn to his love of cars—a film of a sportscar race titled *1:42:08*. The characters are the cars, not the drivers.

In fact, if there was a shortcoming in his resume as a young filmmaker, it was related to Lucas's comfort with machines versus people. He was a shy person—a geek who could fiddle with filmmaking equipment until it delivered the effects he wanted. But people were imprecise. They frustrated him when they failed to catch on to his vision. He developed the habit of going ahead on a set even if his assistants and actors didn't follow what he was doing. He despised writing for the same reasons—he knew what he wanted, and having to spell it out was tedious and boring. Asked about why his early films were more about cool images than characters, Lucas replied, "I did terrible in script writing classes, because I hated script writing. I hated stories, and I hated plot, and I wanted to make visual films that had nothing to do with telling a story."

But filmmaking was the right place for him to be in life—he had no doubts about that. And he had arrived by using a simple method: "Mostly I just followed my inner feelings and passions, and said 'I like this, and I like this,' and I just kept going to where it got warmer and warmer, until it finally got hot, and then that's where I was." He refused to let himself worry about the mysteries of talent and whether or not he had it. A talent, he decided, is "something you can lose yourself in—something that you can start at 9 in the morning, look up from your work and it's 10 o'clock at night—and something that you have a natural ability to do very well. And usually those two things go together."

In 1966 he graduated from USC, having met his goal to finish film school and worry about employment later. Friends and family didn't share his confidence about the future, however, and he heard the discouraging words "You'll never get a job" over and over. Breaking into the entertainment business in Hollywood depended on knowing someone who could get you in. Lucas had instructors who could write recommendations, but he was still just another young person smitten by the movies. Who could get him over the high walls of famous studios? At best, wiser heads told him sadly, he could expect to get into making training films for industry—which paid well, at least.

Fortunately, Lucas did not have his heart set on breaking into Hollywood. It was the mid-'60s, the beginning of the hippie movement, and California was its epicenter. He was into poetry, abstract art, and the lifestyle of an artist. He headed to San Francisco. His film school friends—most of whom stayed in Los Angeles—chalked up his decision to move away from the film capital of the world to further proof that George was a little weird. He kept in touch with them, though, and they tipped each other off to job opportunities, figuring they could crack the system quicker if they helped each other.

Meanwhile, he started work on a highly stylized, science fiction film about the future—*THX-1138: 4EB (Electronic Labyrinth)*. With funds chipped in by family members, Lucas created a 20-minute tale about a cold, antiseptic world where a totalitarian government kept the citizenry under its thumb with drugs and mind games. Once again, Lucas' ability to make images tell a story with minimal dialogue served him exceptionally well this time. *THX-1138: 4EB* won first place at the 1967-68 National Student Film Festival, and Warner Brothers awarded him a scholarship to observe the production of *Finian's Rainbow*.

Lucas, the young filmmaker who said he didn't care if he broke into the entertainment business, was going to Hollywood anyway.

Lucas met Francis Ford Coppola on the set of *Finian's Rainbow*, which Coppola was directing. Despite the differences in their personalities, the two became close and respected each other's artistic vision.

Chapter 4

American Zoetrope and *THX-1138*

"[THX-1138] *was a very personal kind of film and I didn't think [Warner Brothers] had the right to come in and just arbitrarily chop it up at their own whim.*"

—George Lucas

ONLY TWENTY-THREE YEARS old and fresh out of film school, Lucas was pleased that Warner Brothers, one of the most respected and prestigious studios in Hollywood, had offered him a scholarship. What he probably didn't know was that the studio was just as grateful that he had accepted it.

In 1967, Warner Brothers was floundering. Its legendary chief of production, Jack Warner, had left when the company was sold to Seven Arts Entertainment. Since then, the studio had been in deep turmoil. Fear of financial collapse seemed to have cast a permanent chill over the movie giant's creativity. Although Lucas had been offered to chance to see a Warner Brother's movie in production, the irony was that *Finian's Rainbow* was the *only* movie being made on Warner Brother's empty, echoing lots. It was a sadly out-of-date musical starring dancer Fred Astaire, who at that point was a decade past his prime, and Petula Clark, a British pop star. Lucas arrived at Warners Brothers, hopeful to be schooled by a big-time director. He must have been surprised when he discovered the person in the director's chair, Francis Ford Coppola, was only four years older than he was.

The two young men couldn't have been more different. Lucas was skinny and quiet, a straight arrow who dressed in preppy Madras shirts and white jeans. Coppola was a man of big appetites. He was large, outgoing, outspoken, and made no bones about wanting to be one of the most famous directors in film history. He had taken on *Finian's Rainbow* because the money was good. But it was nothing like the edgy, two-fisted movies he planned to make independently. In his opinion, old-fashioned Hollywood studios suffocated talent. Once he got his fee for *Finian's Rainbow*, he said, he was going to be an *auteur*—a French word roughly meaning "film artist."

Lucas and Coppola outwardly presented a complete contrast, but inwardly they shared the same vision. Lucas cherished his right to make his films his way, and Coppola declared that he would never knuckle under to anyone else, either. They became close friends. Coppola promoted Lucas from mere gofer on the set to director's assistant. Then he promised that if Lucas would help with *The Rain People,* the arty film he was doing on the side, Coppola would get Warner Brothers to back a full-length version of Lucas' *THX-1138*. After all, they complemented each other. Lucas knew how to use technology creatively, and Coppola relished big-budget filmmaking in the name of art. They struck a deal to help each other, which cemented the relationship for years to come.

Lucas' private instincts had served him well once again. Just a year earlier, friends and family had been urging him to be more realistic about his future—but now, he couldn't have had a better mentor in his corner. Coppola appreciated him, encouraged him, and showed his shy assistant from Modesto something he absolutely needed to know—how to be a director.

Coppola's gift was working with actors and coaxing their best performances from them. He knew how to make the drama of scripted scenes burst forth on film. He charged out of his chair behind the cameras, interrupting actors in mid-speech to praise, embrace, or scold them. He played his role as director with as much energy and flair as the actors performed their characters. Filmmaking to Coppola was an ecstatic (and sometimes wild) adventure. It was not spelling out pre-decided ideas and themes, or staging someone else's story, which would eventually be shown to an audience like a televised lecture or play. He wanted his films to capture life's energy and unpredictability.

Meanwhile, Lucas' natural reticence was getting him into trouble on the set of *Finian's Rainbow*. He was standoffish, taking in everything and giving little back. Making a film is a risky enterprise, the results of which might shower praise or ridicule on everyone involved. Lucas's lurking around and acting aloof threw cold water on people's spirits. The technical crew in particular, with whom Lucas was supposed to be cooperating, complained directly to Coppola. The director called a special meeting for the sake of damage control. First, he asked for patience from the technical crew on Lucas's behalf. From Lucas, he got a commitment that he would try to be more of a team player. Privately, Coppola took his assistant aside and told him, "You gotta learn how to do this," referring to the skill of interacting with the other members of the crew.

When *Finian's Rainbow* wrapped, Coppola made good on his promise to Lucas and persuaded Warner Brothers to back Lucas in developing *THX* into a feature-length film. By day, Lucas worked on Coppola's *The Rain People*. By night, he labored over turning out a full-fledged script for *THX*. In 1969 when *The Rain People* was completed, Coppola gave his friend one more critical lesson—how to handle money when out from under the thumb of the studio. Or rather, how *not* to handle money.

Flush with cash—some of it borrowed—Coppola took Lucas to Europe on an equipment-buying spree to stock the shelves of their shared dream of having an independent film company. Evidently, Coppola believed that being a real *auteur* meant purchasing equipment where

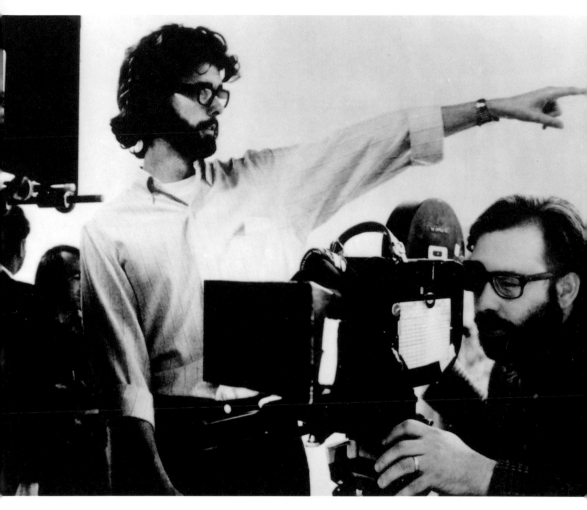

Eventually Coppola showed Lucas how to truly direct people, and later persuaded Warner Brothers to support Lucas' *THX-1138* project in exchange for Lucas working on Coppola's *The Rain People*. The two would also start an independent film company called American Zoetrope.

the big names in independent European filmmaking—Francois Truffaut, Alain Renais, and Federico Fellini, for example—got their equipment. Pulling Lucas behind him like a little boat in his expansive wake, Coppola recklessly and lavishly purchased cameras, editing equipment, and sound equipment, ignoring Lucas' pleas to slow down.

Returning to the United States and loaded with hardware, they rented a warehouse in San Francisco. They dubbed their company American Zoetrope after one of the earliest motion picture devices. For hours, they would cheerfully discuss how it would become a community of writers, producers, and directors, turning out emotionally honest films, not the dross mass-produced by Hollywood. But their first project, of course, would be the one dearest to Lucas' heart—*THX-1138*. Adding to his happiness, Lucas married Marcia Griffin, a film editor, on February 22.

While the financial and creative pieces for *THX-1138* fell into place, Lucas landed a gig as a technician on a project that would become a minor classic—Al and David Maysles' 1970 Rolling Stones documentary, *Gimme Shelter*. The film captures the tumult of the 1960s with a Woodstock-like outdoor concert in Altamont, California. It records the excesses of the era, too. When a Stones' fan at the edge of the stage threatens the band, a bodyguard platoon of Hell's Angels beats him to death. Lucas kept the cameras rolling the whole time.

With Warner Brothers' money and Coppola's supervision, Lucas was soon ready to begin shooting *THX-1138*. It was his first time directing a major motion picture. In the male lead was a young actor eager for work, Robert Duvall, who played the character named THX-1138.

The story is set in an underground world of the future where sex is outlawed. A repressive government manufactures the population in laboratories. To maintain order, the masses are force fed sedatives to keep them passive. But THX-1138 and his lover LUH-3417 rebel—

THX-1138 stops taking the drugs and LUH-3417 becomes pregnant. They flee, but government forces capture them and consign them to White Limbo, a jail where inmates are contained by their own fear. With the help of others, THX-1138 escapes alone, eventually reaching the surface and freedom.

Despite being young and having no clout in Hollywood, Lucas made the film his way, sticking to his conviction that he should remain independent. "I liked non-story, non-character tone poems that were being done in San Francisco at that time," he said, and the film strongly reflects that influence. Tone poems rely on abrupt, contrasting images to create feelings in the reader. Lucas went for a similar effect by using sparse dialogue, black and white settings, and blunt editing that jumped from one scene to the next without warning. Said Steven Spielberg about Lucas' distinctive style of cutting film, "George makes his visuals come to life with montage. That makes him unique in our generation, since most of us do it instead with composition and camera placement." The on-location shoot lasted 40 days in the San Francisco Bay area. Lucas, ever money-conscious, completed the entire Technicolor film for only $777,000—much less than the fee commanded today by major actors for their performances alone.

But when *THX-1138* was screened at Warner Brothers, the studio's executives were outraged. The film did not follow standard narrative style, did not delve into character, and contained dialogue that seemed to have been written for telegrams. The images were striking, it was true—and the concept could even be judged first-rate science fiction—but Warner Brothers wanted a blockbuster like Stanley Kubrick's *2001: A Space*

Odyssey, not an arty film for college students. Over Lucas' protests, the film was recut by Warner Brothers editors and granted little fanfare when it was dropped into theaters in 1971. Lucas never got over how the film was treated at the hands of studio higher-ups. "It was a very personal kind of film and I didn't think they had the right to come in and just arbitrarily chop it up at their own whim."

THX-1138 flopped but attracted a cult of admirers, some of whom maintain that it is still his best film to date, presenting remarkable images and a minimum of special effects. Moreover, in a number of ways, the film is a blueprint for all his future work.

First, there are three themes in *THX-1138* that also appear in Lucas' later films—how people can escape repression through accepting responsibility; how deeply humanity is involved with machines; and how hard work leads to success (one of Lucas's personal mottoes is "Talent without hard work doesn't get you very far.")

Second, his fascination with pitting good against evil comes through, as well. Returning to the "good guys versus the bad guys" westerns of his boyhood, Lucas has the good guys wear white and the bad guys wear black. THX-1138 and LUH-3417 wear white costumes in dark, foreboding underground settings. Years later, black-armored Darth Vader confronts Luke Skywalker and Princess Leia, both garbed in white. Another good versus evil parallel is that THX-1138 defies a malevolent government, and Luke and his companions take on the Empire.

And third, despite the dismal future portrayed in *THX-1138*, Lucas insists on being hopeful, another hallmark

Lucas' pet project *THX-1138* finally became a feature-length film star-ring Robert Duvall in 1971. Although it flopped and remained a sore point for Lucas because of the studio's handling of the editing and publicity, Lucas fans consider it an impressive film and see in it a foreshadowing of the *Star Wars* films.

of all his later films. Film critic Charles Champlain in *George Lucas: The Creative Impulse* points out that *THX-1138* reveals "the essential warmth of [Lucas'] prevailing view – innocent, imaginative, and, despite all that he found alarming in society, finally optimistic." The message of *THX*, in Lucas' own words, could stand for all his *Star Wars* films: "If we're not careful about the way we conduct our lives, we're going to live in a society devoid of pain and risk, but insulated, emotionless, and much more unpleasant." In the final moments of *THX* (Lucas the former car racer couldn't resist adding an exciting car chase climax to the film) Robert Duvall emerges from underground and is greeted by a glorious sunrise.

The sunrise at the end could just as well have been a metaphor for Lucas' own struggle to free himself from studio pressure. He resented that Warner Brothers had bullied him about *THX-1138*, and as his first feature-length movie ended its short run in theaters, he retaliated by incorporating Lucasfilm, Ltd. Although only a production company on paper at the time, Lucasfilm, Ltd. was a statement—his commitment to becoming an independent filmmaker, years before the style became fashionable in Hollywood.

Almost at the same time, unfortunately, American Zoetrope began to fall apart. Coppola's spending spree had put the two young *auteurs* behind the eight-ball from the beginning. Warner Brothers, fearing that no blockbusters would be coming out of Zoetrope anytime soon, pulled its financing and saddled Coppola with a personal debt of $300,000. Lucas bitterly interpreted the move as yet another example of Hollywood's fickleness. The partners were forced to split apart, with Coppola hanging on to the remains of Zoetrope. Reluctantly, Coppola agreed to direct a gangster melodrama that seemed like a throwback to the 1940s—*The Godfather*, based on an unpublished novel by Mario Puzo. Ironically, it would be one of his most successful films ever.

Meanwhile, Lucas concentrated on developing his idea for another film, one with a twin emphasis on entertainment and quality. If he had to get money to finance his own projects, so be it. He could make a film that would pull in mainstream moviegoers, too.

He buckled down by creating a low-budget movie that could play in drive-ins as well as suburban theaters. It would be called *American Graffiti*.

American Graffiti would take Lucas back to the time period of his youth, as well as be a stylistic homage to the movies he enjoyed then. It was also his first major success that launched his filmmaking career and made him a millionaire.

Chapter **5**

American Graffiti

[American Graffiti] *was about my life as I grew up, so I cared about it a lot.*

—George Lucas

IN 1971, THE VIETNAM WAR—the political and foreign policy misadventure that cost 55,000 American lives—was stumbling toward an end. Just ten years before, the country had been in a mood of optimism and hope. President John F. Kennedy had proclaimed, "We choose to go to the moon."

Liberal thinkers looked forward to a dramatic change in society that would bring about racial, economic, and gender equality. Youth, especially the teen years, was a period of excitement and exploration in American life.

As George Lucas set to work in that year on the film that would become *American Graffiti*, he returned to America of ten years before, as well as his own adolescence, to recapture those happier times.

On the one hand, a film that would portray small-town high school hijinks on a weekend night in northern California was creatively risky—some might even have called it irresponsible. A number of young filmmakers Lucas's age were flinging the country's shortcomings and hypocrisies in the face of movie audiences. Their films raged about official corruption, campus demonstrations, racism, and corporate greed. Would a lightweight film about drag racing, rock 'n' roll, finding a boyfriend or girlfriend, and growing up be welcome in theaters, or ridiculed?

On the other hand, perhaps the mood of the country was weary and nostalgic, which would create a solid market for a film that had no other purpose than to entertain and remind moviegoers of another era. Lucas bet the latter was really the case. Once again, it was a matter of believing his instincts were correct.

The first problem, the same one faced by all filmmakers who want to maintain their independence from studios, was raising the money to make the movie. He wrote a treatment, or summary, of what *American Graffiti* would be about. "I've always been interested in that theme of leaving an environment or facing change, and how kids do it," and that would be at the heart of the movie, he decided. His characters, four teenage boys, would have to choose whether to remain dependent on the past, or move on to accepting the future and adult responsibilities. With his treatment in hand, he went off to Europe in search of investors. With the problems that had dogged *THX-1138* in Hollywood, he probably figured he would get a better reception abroad.

At the Cannes Film Festival, he found the money he needed to get going. But he was still struggling with, as he called it, "my 'I don't want to be a writer syndrome,'" so he contacted two friends back home to write the screenplay. Earlier, they told him they were interested, but now it turned out they weren't, because they were busy with their own low-budget film. It was the first monkey wrench in the project. Unable to return to the United States for three months because of various commitments, Lucas hooked up with a producer who promised to get the screenplay written, but the price would be all the money Lucas had raised so far. The capital Lucas had in hand was "so tiny," he felt he had no choice.

Returning to California from England, he received the completed screenplay and proceeded to read it. He was shocked, angry, and disappointed: "the screenplay was completely different from the story treatment. It was more like 'hotrods to hell.' It was very fantasy-like, with playing chicken and things that kids didn't really do. I wanted something that was more like the way I grew up." The screenplay, in effect, was worthless.

Now all the money was gone and he had wasted time. In a sense, he was less far along than he had been months earlier. Facing the inevitable, he sat down to write the screenplay himself. If it were ever to reach theater screens, he realized, it was going to have to be the first movie from Lucasfilm, Ltd. from start to finish.

He remembered it in an interview with the American Academy of Achievement as "a very dark period":

> I had all these producers calling me saying, 'I hear you're really good at material that doesn't have a story. I've got a record album I want you to make into a movie.' Or, you know, things like that. And they were offering me a lot of money and—but they were terrible projects. And so . . . I had to constantly turn down vast sums of money while I was starving, writing a screenplay for free that I didn't like to write, because I hated writing . . . . [but] you simply have to say, 'This is what I want to do. I want to make my movie. I don't want to take the money.' And you just walk forward, step by step, and get through it somehow. And I got through. It actually only took me about three weeks to write that script. I just every day would sit down at eight o'clock in the morning and I'd write until about eight o'clock at night. And I just said, 'I'm going to finish this, as painful as it is, and I'm going to ignore these phone calls of lure of riches and get through this.' And somehow I did it.

He did not comfort himself with the illusion, either, that great art was pouring out from his pencil. He was trying to write a "B movie," as movies that are low-budget, plot-heavy, and crowd-pleasing are commonly called. *American Graffiti* would be in the style of "teenage hot rod movies made by American International Pictures, which were sort of the lowest rung of the movie ladder," he said. But he had loved that type of picture as a boy. This time around, his version would be distinguished by the quality of filmmaking. No awkwardness or lack of professionalism would mar the experience of watching.

He put more into it than perhaps even he realized. "It was about my life as I grew up, so I cared about it a lot,"

Although Lucas can expertly handle most aspects of the film-making process, he has always felt uncomfortable with script writing. Unfortunately, he found the screenplay he had hired someone else to write for *American Graffiti* to be completely different from what he had envisioned the movie to be, so he reluctantly wrote it himself.

Lucas admitted. To capture the euphoria and excitement of being a teenager with his whole life ahead of him, Lucas took the unusual step of intertwining four different stories, all taking place simultaneously—a night at the end of summer—experienced four different ways. Although that method of storytelling has since become standard fare on television programs, it was not often seen in theaters 30 years ago.

When he finished the first draft, he called on help from two USC classmates to polish the screenplay. They added humor and deepened the characters to make them more sympathetic. For months, the threesome worked on revisions, crafting a movie that could not fail to engage the hearts of moviegoers—though they knew it probably wouldn't find favor with the minds of critics. Then they began marketing the completed screenplay to studios.

American International Pictures nearly signed on, recognizing the kind of picture they had succeeded so well with in the 1950s and 60s. But then they backed off, bothered by the four stories unfolding instead of one linear story about a group of guys and girls in cars. Instead, Universal Pictures, another Hollywood kingdom of B movies, bought it with Lucas as director. Filming got underway in Marin and Sonoma Counties in California in late 1972, featuring a cast of actors—some relatively unknown at the time—that included Ron Howard, Richard Dreyfuss, and Harrison Ford. Lucas, characteristically watching the bottom line, completed shooting in 28 days at a cost of $775,000. Editing and sound engineering was completed at American Zoetrope studios in San Francisco.

In *American Graffiti,* a night in 1962 becomes the focal point in the lives of four small town California teenagers as they face decisions—both immediate and long-term—about the directions of their lives. Steve wants to break up with Laurie, his devoted high school sweetheart, and pursue new experiences away from home. Curt is hesitant about going away to school and leaving the comfortable, familiar surroundings of family and friends. John tries to maintain his "too cool to care" image as a drag racer, but can't seem to shake a nagging awareness that life is somehow passing him by. Finally, there's Terry, who's nicknamed Toad, the nerdy wannabe who wants to fit in but can't unwind long enough to let his own story happen. During the course of the evening, their individual stories intertwine and separate. By the next morning, their lives are changed, some temporarily and some forever.

The film premiered in August, 1973. By year's end, it had grossed a whopping $145 million, or $50 for every dollar invested—a ratio that not even any of the *Star Wars* films would equal. Nominated for Best Picture and Best Original Screenplay Academy Awards, the movie's rock 'n' roll hits and haunting street sounds at night raised soundtracks to new levels of importance, financially and artistically.

"[It] was a big moment for me," Lucas said. He was now able to say to himself, "Okay, now I am a director. Now I know I can get a job. I can work in this industry, and apply my trade, and express my ideas on things. and be creative in a way that I enjoy. . . . There wasn't anything in my life that was going to stop me from making movies."

When Lucas had first applied to film school, his father objected, saying that his son needed to be more realistic about his choice of careers. Lucas countered by predicting that he would be a millionaire before he turned 30. Thanks to the success of *American Graffiti*, Lucas beat his own prediction by two years. By 28, he was a millionaire.

But he barely allowed himself to take the time to enjoy

A drag-racing scene from *American Graffiti*. With the money Lucas made from the success of *American Graffiti*, he was able to start three companies—Lucasfilm, THX, and Industrial Light & Magic.

the success of *American Graffiti*. He plowed the profits into his business, Lucasfilm, and two new companies—THX, a research and development company for theater sound, and Industrial Light & Magic, a special effects company that would later master the animation action in movies such as *Jurassic Park* and *The Lost World*.

And he was already at work on a much larger film-making project—one about the far future and a distant galaxy. It would take place in episodes like old Saturday movie serials. To heighten the drama, the first episode would actually be the middle of the series. The working title was "Star Wars."

When friends heard about the scope of the *Star Wars* series, Lucas remembered them saying, "Boy! Watch out, boy. When that one hits you're really going be thrown for a loop."

He replied, "Oh, no-no. I went through *American Graffiti*. I can handle this."

Mark Hamill as Luke Skywalker in one of the opening scenes of *Star Wars*. Lucas wrote the saga in the vein of classic mythology and added science-fiction elements from his favorite movie and TV serials.

Chapter **6**

The Saga

I would rather see us be a positive force in the universe than a cancer. We have the knowledge to be either one. That, in essence, is what Star Wars *is about. We are both good and evil, and we have a choice.*

—George Lucas

THE SUCCESS OF *American Graffiti* convinced Lucas that he had been right. Despite social unrest caused by the Vietnam War, audiences had flocked to see an upbeat film that left them feeling good. The same principle had worked during the Great Depression in the 1930s. Even then, theatergoers who could barely afford the price of a movie ticket still went in droves to see lavish musicals and melodramas that made them forget their cares for a while.

Lucas decided to continue in a similar direction, but that would mean bucking the trend of 1970s Hollywood. The best pictures of the decade—directed by Robert Altman, Francis Ford Coppola, Martin Scorsese, Sam Peckinpah, Brian De Palma, Bob Fosse and others—depicted realism in films, not escapist fun. There were violent gangster movies: *The Godfather*, *Mean Streets*, and *Thieves Like Us*; detective movies: *The Long Goodbye*, and *The Late Show*; gloomy westerns: *McCabe and Mrs. Miller*, and *The Return of a Man Called Horse*; and films about human failings with unhappy endings: *Watergate, Taxi Driver, Carrie, The Last Picture Show*, and *One Flew Over the Cuckoo's Nest*, for instance. They were serious, often shocking, and aimed at adults.

Nevertheless, Lucas believed, "You can learn from cynicism, but you can't build on it." Films like *The Godfather* exposed audiences to the vices of the underworld, but left them feeling anxious, unsettled. The secret to *American Graffiti*, he maintained, was that serious themes about responsibility and growing-up were embedded in a highly entertaining film.

Having based *American Graffiti* on one of his favorite categories of movies—B-movie hot rod pictures from the 1950s—he turned to his youth again for inspiration. This time he would draw on some of his favorite movie and TV serials—ones about outer space such as *Flash Gordon* and *Adventure Theater*. But again, he would add an element of seriousness, just as he had to *American Graffiti*.

He would tap into humanity's love of heroes. He would send heroes taken from fairy tales, fables, and mythology to battle high-tech monsters and machines in outer space— sort of "Jason and the Argonauts versus the Martians."

Even as *American Graffiti* was still playing in theaters in 1973, he set to work. Immediately, however, his old dislike of scriptwriting plagued him again. He hired a team of writers he hoped could translate his vision of an eye-popping space opera to paper. But he was dissatisfied with the results, just as he had been when he hired someone else to script *American Graffiti*. Reluctantly, he confronted the blank page himself. (A perfectionist who dislikes delegating authority, Lucas was still fine-tuning *Star Wars: Episode IV*, the first in the series, two-and-a-half years later, right up to its release. He excuses himself by saying, "I come up from the filmmakers' school of doing movies, which means I do everything myself.")

His first concern was what borrow from fairytales, fables, and mythology for his screenplay. He read deeply in anthropology, drawing heavily on Joseph Campbell's book, *The Hero with a Thousand Faces*, which explains the traits of the hero as a type in many cultures. Lucas decided to stick with the noblest human ideals, "the folk side of things," as he called it, avoiding sex and violence. "My films aren't that violent or that sexy. Instead, I'm dealing with the need for humans to have friendships, to be compassionate, to band together to help each other and to join together against what is negative."

Asked in an interview about whether his interests are typical of what a filmmaker needs, Lucas said, "What you've really got to do is focus on learning as much about life, and about various aspects of it first. Then learn the techniques of making a movie, because that stuff you can pick up pretty quickly. But having a really good understanding of history, literature, psychology, sciences is very, very important to actually being able to make movies."

In fact, when boiled down to its basic outline, the plot of *Star Wars: Episode IV* sounds very much like an child-appropriate fairy tale: In a distant galaxy, a long time ago, young Luke Skywalker assembles his motley crew of allies including space rogue Han Solo and two "droids"—C3PO and R2D2—to rescue Princess Leia, the rebel leader of her planet from the clutches of the evil Empire, represented its enforcer Darth Vader. Change Luke and Han to knights on horseback, and Darth Vader to a dragon, and most children would recognize the basic storyline. Lucas apparently felt so confident about the general direction of the plot that he didn't bother to "flesh out the storyline . . . I had a rough of idea of what happened and who the major characters were, but I didn't include a scene-by-scene scenario of what happened in my treatment." Even so, he realized that he had enough material not for one movie, but several. *Star Wars* was shaping up to be a hero's long journey, like the ancient tales it emulated.

But despite its classic story elements, *Star Wars* had a rough time finding a major studio to finance it. First, the genre or creative category was science fiction, and for that reason alone some studio executives backed away. Science fiction was strictly old hat, uncommercial, with only three exceptions: *Fantastic Voyage*; *2001: A Space Odyssey*; and *Planet of the Apes*—all based on popular novels. Second, Lucas had strange characters in major roles—robots and a Wookie, for instance. Traditionally, robots were dumb helpers, not humanoids with hopes and fears. Third, the concept seemed aimed at children, which brought the complaint, as Lucas remembered it, "Look, that's Disney's.

Lucas was up against the studio's doubts about *Star Wars'* possible success—science fiction wasn't seen as a very commercial genre, and Lucas would be introducing a completely original storyline that no one was familiar with beforehand.

Disney does that. The rest of us can't do that, so we don't want to get into that area." And fourth, the storyline was too long. Lucas clearly had several movies in mind, and no studio was willing it take the risk.

Finally, however, 20th Century Fox—taking the attitude that Lucas had been right with *American Graffiti* and might produce a hit again—agreed to sign on. But there was no deal to make more than one movie. To himself, Lucas vowed, "Okay. I'll get rid of the last two thirds of it, and I'll just do the first act. I can make that into one movie. . . . I'm not going to give this up. I won't just put this on the shelf and forget it. I'll make this into three movies and I will make all three movies." In exchange for turning down a director's salary, he agreed to accept more of the financial risk himself. He would get 40 percent of the box office gross—whatever that turned out to be—plus merchandising rights. But in keeping with his personal pledge to make all three movies, he snapped up sequel rights, though skeptics at 20th Century Fox probably thought there wouldn't be any sequels.

Lucas readily admits that the kinds of financial and creative difficulties he experienced with his first two full-length movies—*THX-1138* and *American Graffiti*—did not suddenly disappear when he undertook the *Star Wars* series. "Film is not an easy occupation," he said in an interview. "There's a lot of occupations that are difficult and film is one of them. There's always adversity that you're faced with. I like to tell students that I talk to that, you know, it's not a matter of how well can you make a movie. It's how well can you make it under the circumstances, because there's always circumstances and you cannot use that as an excuse. . . . You simply have to show them the movie and it has got to work, and there are no excuses. And so you really have to focus on what you're doing and just plow ahead no matter what hurdles are thrown in front of you."

Behind the scenes, he began putting in place the technology he would need to realize his dream of what *Star Wars* would look and sound like. There were no studio production units capable of creating the kind of special effects the film demanded. So in 1975, Lucas gathered a team of talented young artists, designers, and technicians together to build a new company, Industrial Light & Magic. Another company, Sprocket Systems (renamed Skywalker Sound in 1989), was set up to edit and mix the film.

Then in mid-1976, it was off to Tunisia to begin on-location shooting without the cast.

He had directed Harrison Ford in *American Graffiti*, and English actor Alec Guinness was one of the most famous leading men on stage and screen of his generation. But most of the cast and crew were strangers to Lucas. His shyness, misinterpreted as aloofness, caught up with him once again, causing morale problems. A technician on the crew complained that the director knew what he wanted, but "the problem was that none of us knew what that was." The cast also expressed bewilderment at Lucas's minimal direction. Mark Hamill, who played the role of Luke Skywalker, later told an interviewer, "I have a sneaking suspicion that if there were a way to make movies without actors, George would do it." Moreover, lines in the script sounded stiff and unbelievable. "I thought I recognized your foul stench when I came aboard," says Carrie Fischer as Princess Leia, sounding like a prim heroine in a school play. Harrison Ford told Lucas bluntly, "You can type this [expletive] George, but you sure can't say it." Lucas wasn't enjoying himself either. "I had to direct 500 people on *Star Wars*," he remembers, "and I hated it. I accept the power to do whatever I like with my camera. But I refuse to command other people."

After ten days, shooting ended in Tunisia, right on schedule. The raw footage went to England, where an editor whom Lucas hardly knew cut the scenes. With a sinking heart, Lucas watched the early scenes and realized "they just weren't working, and I was very down about the whole situation." Was he failing as a director? he wondered. On several Sundays in a row, he went into the cutting room alone and recut the scenes. The British editor, he discovered, had stopped the action about a foot a film before he would have made a cut. The extra seconds made all the difference.

Shooting continued on indoor sets in England where Lucas assumed everyone would work as late as necessary until a scene came out right. But British union crewmembers behaved otherwise. They quit for tea in late afternoon and generally quit for the day very early. Then, out of the blue, studio executives at 20th Century Fox decided it was time to pull the plug on financing. Lucas received a directive telling him to collapse two weeks' of work into three days. Desperate, he hired triple crews and divided the stage into three sets, rushing back and forth to direct the action. By the end of shooting he was pale and ill.

But the worst was yet to come. Returning to Los Angeles where Lucasfilm was then headquartered, he was speechless with anger to find that the special effects unit had blown half its $2 million budget on three shots. He took control of the operation, then flew home to San Francisco, supposedly for a rest. Instead he began having chest pains and was taken to Marin General Hospital. The diagnosis was exhaustion. He later told biographer Dale Pollock, "That's when I really confirmed to myself that I was going to change. I wasn't going to make more films, I wasn't going to direct anymore. I was going to get my life a bit more under control."

But the work had to go on. On the positive side, *Star Wars* was now going into a strictly technological production phase, which Lucas always enjoyed. He met with sound expert Ben Burtt and told him he wanted an "organic" soundtrack. "Since we were going to design a visual world that had rust and dents and dirt," Burtt said in an interview in *Film Sound Today*, "we wanted a sound which had squeaks and motors that may not be smooth-sounding or quiet. Therefore we wanted to draw upon raw material from

Lucas entrusted the creation of the sounds effects in *Star Wars* to sound expert Ben Burtt. One effect he achieved was blending the sounds of a television set and a 35mm film projector to achieve the lightsaber's hum.

the real world: real motors, real squeaky door, real insects, this sort of thing."

To create the sound of Imperial Walkers, Burtt modified the sound of a machinist's punch press and added the noise of bicycle chains being dropped on concrete. The screech of a TIE Fighter came from a drastically altered elephant bellow. Wookie sounds were assembled from pieces of walrus and other animal vocalizations. To create a piercing yet rever-berating laser blast, Burtt struck an antenna tower guy wire with a hammer. Ironically, the hum of a light saber far in the future is really the blended sounds of Burtt's 20th century TV and an old 35mm projector. But perhaps the most ingenious sound—the noise of Luke Skywalker's landspeeder—

comes from recording the roar of the Los Angeles Harbor Freeway through a vacuum-cleaner pipe.

For his on-screen hardware, Lucas relied on technicians to fabricate scuffed-up and oily mechanical devices, not the kind of gleaming gadgets usually seen in films about outer space. The goal was to create reality, not a Hollywood stage universe. Under their hands, $30,000 worth of scrap metal and junk—including jet engines and pipes—was fashioned into unique vehicles, machines, and weapons. For his alien beings, Lucas turned to a London firm called Uglies, Ltd. to produce creatures with trunklike noses, cobra heads and furry chins.

When *Star Wars: Episode IV: A New Hope* (known simply as *Star Wars*) was released on May 25, 1977 audiences were mesmerized by what they saw. As Roger Ebert explained in his review, "the events in the movie seem real, and I seem to be a part of them . . . On whatever level (sometimes I'm not at all sure) they engage me so immediately and powerfully that I lose my detachment, my analytical reserve. The movie's happening, and it's happening to me."

From a technical standpoint, among Lucas' most outstanding achievements were implementing increased frame rates and the use of optical zooms to create the illusion of lightspeed space travel. In addition, to enhance the detail in special effects, he avoided the graininess of 35mm film and went instead to the giant 70mm format used mainly for screen spectaculars in the early 1960s. The work of the Industrial Light and Magic team quickly became the industry standard for its seamless visual effects.

Completed on a budget of $10 million, *Star Wars* grossed $400 million in its initial run, not counting profits from toys, comic books, and other collectibles. Until *Star Wars*, in fact, the practice of merchandising goods connected with a

Star Wars also saw remarkable success in licensing toys, and the original ones are worth amounts many times above their original price. In 1999, the toymaker Hasbro reissued some of the original figures as well as new ones from *The Phantom Menace*.

movie was practically unknown. Only Disney had aggressively promoted characters as toys and games. "As it turned out," said Lucas, "[*Star Wars*] was so successful we were able to make toy deals and we began to start the whole idea of action figures, of tie-ins, of toys that go along with movies. Over the years that's one of the things that's helped me stay independent and finance my own movies and stay in business." In 2000, *Star Wars* action figures were the top selling toys for boys, second overall to Barbie. Some of the original plastic action figures, which sold for about $3 in 1978, are now valued at $1,400 and over.

At the Academy Awards ceremony in the spring of 1978, *Star Wars* received six Academy Awards for original score, film editing, sound, art and set decoration, costume design and visual effects, as well as Special Achievement Academy Award for sound effects creations.

But not everyone who saw the movie was enchanted, or thought the honors granted it were deserved. There were critics who disliked it immediately, and others who have since detested its influence on the film industry.

In the *New Yorker* magazine, Pauline Kael condemned "The loudness, the smash-and-grab editing, the relentless pacing drive every idea from your head." *Star Wars*, she wrote, "has no emotional grip." Said John Baxter, who later wrote a biography of Lucas, "God, it was so mindless." Most negative reviews faulted Lucas for sacrificing development of theme and character to edge-of-your-seat action.

As recently as 2001, film critic Jason Ankeny echoed the complaint of many film lovers who look back over the last 25 years and realize that *Star Wars* shoved aside thoughtful filmmaking meant to engage audience's minds, and replaced it with candy for their eyes:

> [*Star Wars*] effectively ended a renaissance in American filmmaking, shifting the focus away from the personal, character-driven films of directors like [Francis Ford] Coppola, Martin Scorsese and Robert Altman to action-packed, special effects-powered events . . . . The most notable aspect of the picture's storytelling was its breakneck pacing, edited by Lucas himself in tandem with his wife. Seemingly no film had ever moved so quickly, and its overwhelming success proved not only that a generation weaned on the rapid pace of television could easily absorb such an onslaught of image and sound, but that this was the kind of narrative they wanted to see on a regular basis.

Studios scrambled to produce thrill-a-minute movies,

calling for screenplays pitched at the level of middle-school audiences, a trend that continues to the present day. Films of this type used to be the fare at theaters on Saturdays only for kids. Now action-heavy films featuring expensive special effects routinely make up what's offered to adults. In an article appearing in *Salon.com,* "How 'Star Wars' Ruined American Movies," Charles Taylor accuses Lucas of having brought about "the infantilization of movies." Said Lucas about his influence in putting spectacle over ideas in movies, "I'm a filmmaker, not a director. I like the physical part of making movies. I might be a toymaker if I wasn't a filmmaker."

Immediately on the heels of *Star Wars'* success, plans shifted into high gear for the second installment of the *Star Wars* series, *The Empire Strikes Back.* But Lucas had no interest in directing it because of his unhappy experiences with the previous movie. The reins were handed to Irvin Kershner, whose 30-year resumé as a director includes *The Hoodlum Priest, Loving*, and *The Return of a Man Called Horse.* Widely considered the best of the Star Wars movies so far, Kershner treats the characters as human beings, not as mythology types. Chewbacca wails as he holds C-3PO's head in his hands; Luke is clearly afraid when he confronts Darth Vader alone. In addition, the cinematography gives the movie a dark, foreboding feeling adding to the drama. It was a hit in 1980, ending with a cliffhanger that prepared audiences for the third movie in the trilogy, *The Return of the Jedi*, slated for release in 1983.

While *The Return of the Jedi* was in production, Lucas teamed up with former USC classmate Steven Spielberg to release another huge hit, *Raiders of the Lost Ark*, starring Harrison Ford. *Raiders* became the first in another film serial, the Indiana Jones series, followed by the 1984 sequel

Even though Lucas had already written most of the entire storyline for the *Star Wars* saga, it was only *Star Wars'* immense success that allowed the rest of the sequels (and prequels) to be made.

Indiana Jones and the Temple of Doom. Despite complaints that *Temple of Doom* contained graphic violence, Lucas and Spielberg insisted it be granted a rating for teenage audiences. The industry bowed and created a new rating, PG-13, which made the movie available to Lucas's target audience. In Britain, however, censors demanded 25 cuts before the film could be seen by children under 16. Said Steven Schiff in *Vanity Fair* magazine, "It's useless to pretend that *Indiana Jones and the Temple of Doom* isn't upsetting. And it's useless to pretend that the people it upsets most are children." The series continued with *Indiana Jones and the Last Crusade* in 1989.

In 1983, audiences caught the last of the *Star Wars* trilogy with the release of *The Return of the Jedi*. But fourteen years later in 1997, Lucas whetted the appetites of *Star Wars* fans again by re-releasing the trilogy with digitally remastered soundtracks, restored prints, enhanced visual effects and newly added footage. One episode in the original series went into theaters every other month that spring.

Two years later, the latest installment in the *Star Wars* saga appeared. Cult followers and avid fans stood eagerly in line for *Star Wars* prequel, *Episode 1: The Phantom Menace*, starring Liam Neeson, Ewan McGregor and Natalie Portman. After a series of premiere screenings that raised $5.6 million for charity, *The Phantom Menace* opened to record-breaking business across North America, ending the year with ticket sales of $400 million. The film received front-page hype in newspapers, but a lukewarm response for audiences and critics.

The will be six *Star Wars* films in all. The next prequel, *Star Wars: Episode II: The Attack of the Clones* was released in 2002. *Star Wars: Episode III* isn't expected till 2005.

The Skywalker Ranch is a facility that Lucas built in Marin County to house his companies—a very ambitious and expensive undertaking. At one point, it cost $20 million a year just to keep the Ranch running.

Chapter 7

George Lucas, the Industry

"I've never focused on making the money. I've always focused on not losing the money."

—George Lucas

THE RELEASE OF *The Return of the Jedi* in 1983, the third installment in the trilogy, brought to an end an important period in Lucas's life.

That year, he filed for divorce from his wife of 18 years,

Marcia Griffin, a film editor, eventually sharing joint custody of their three adopted children. In 1984, he announced he was stepping down from actively managing Lucasfilm for two years, saying, "I've put up with *Star Wars* taking over, pushing itself into first position, for too long." Privately, he told friends he wanted to spend more time with his children. In an attempt to soften the impact of his withdrawal, Lucas's managers at Lucasfilm and Industrial Light & Magic (ILM) asked for the authority to direct company films. According to one of Lucas's biographers, John Baxter, Lucas told them there was room for only one filmmaker in his organization.

Nevertheless, he seemed weary of being responsible for big-budget features. Instead he concentrated on constructing Skywalker Ranch in Marin County in Northern California, a facility he custom-designed to accommodate the creative, technical, and administrative needs of his companies. Eventually, Skywalker Ranch would include a 150,000-square-foot post-production and music recording facility as well as offices used for the research and development of new technologies in editing, audio, and multimedia.

The costs would be enormous. Moreover, when his divorce was finalized in 1985, he agreed to pay his ex-wife $100 million. Lucas began looking for ways to consolidate his money. In 1983, ILM's computer division had split into Lucasfilm Games and Pixar. The games division became self-supporting almost immediately. But Pixar, which was devoted to experimenting with fully digitalized films, was an expensive research and development operation. Based on how costly it had been to run, Lucas decided he wouldn't make a computer-generated *Star Wars* and sold Pixar in 1985 to Steven Jobs, the founder of Apple computer, for $10 million.

As it turned out, Lucas had unknowingly created a fierce competitor. Jobs invested $50 million during the next ten years to refine high-end computer animation. In 1997, Pixar created the first completely computer generated feature, *Toy Story*, and developed Renderman, a graphics program that generated the dinosaurs in *Jurassic Park*. Other companies also exploited ILM's breakthrough technologies Lucas had resisted patenting. Eventually, ILM was forced to purchase Renderman from Pixar or fall behind in the race to improve Computer Graphics Images (CGI). Nonetheless, Lucas has insisted he has no regrets about selling off Pixar, saying, "ILM is exactly like Pixar, except we don't do animated movies. We do animated pieces in feature films. I didn't need two companies that were doing the same thing."

More interesting to him—from a technological standpoint, anyway—was the development of sound for movies. For the premier of *The Return of the Jedi* in 1983, Lucasfilm pioneered in two special theaters its THX System for high quality presentation, named for Lucas's first feature, *THX-1138*. In 1986, Lucasfilm began research on the Home THX audio system.

But the longer Lucas stayed away from the day-today operations of Lucasfilm to pursue his own projects, the more the company drifted. Annual sales of *Star Wars* toys, estimated at $150 million in 1981, dropped to $50 million by 1986. Meanwhile, the number of employees at Lucasfilm ballooned to 800. Just keeping the Ranch running cost $20 million a year. Lucas returned to take control in 1986, complaining, "I'd go off to make movies and come back two years later and find everybody had hired an assistant." Lucas appointed a new president, Doug Norby, to help him get things back on track. Norby suggested they make deep cuts and Lucas agreed. Twenty-five of the 450 staffers who worked on-site at the Ranch were laid off, and ten departments were trimmed in size—legal, publicity, personnel, marketing, and the art and photo libraries. Within a year, the payroll was down to 400 employees.

That problem addressed, Lucas returned to a personal project: executive-producing Disneyland's 3-D musical space adventure *Captain Eo,* starring Michael Jackson and directed by Francis Ford Coppola. The 17-minute special effects spectacular premiered in 1986 in a Disneyland theater designed by Lucas, ILM, and Disney. Lucas also developed *Star Tours*, combining the technology of a flight simulator with ILM special effects, which became the most popular attraction at Disneyland.

To onlookers in the business world, however, too much of the success of Lucasfilm seemed to depend on the mood, creativity, and ambitions of Lucas himself. Business analyst Michael Cloply commented in the *Wall Street Journal* that Lucas was an un-businesslike businessman, remote from the reality of profit and loss and clinging to a dream of independence that "has been increasingly undermined by a cult of personality that threatens to stifle creativity and excellence."

Almost prophetically, Lucasfilm stumbled. 1986's *Howard the Duck*, based on a cult hit from Marvel Comics, was both a critical and commercial bomb, and 1988's sword-and-sorcery epic *Willow* fared little better. Lucas had insisted from the start that *Willow*—his answer to the popularity of J.R.R. Tolkien's *Hobbit* and *Lord of the Rings* novels—was not a special effects movie. But he commissioned 400 special effects from ILM, creating a sense of confusion among the staff. Said Michael McAllister, an ILM effects supervisor, that if *Willow* had been someone else's movie, Lucasfilm would never have signed on.

Willow was a Lucasfilm project that featured morphing technology developed by the crew at ILM. Unfortunately, Lucas never patented the technology, and ILM became a company installing impressive special effects in other company's sub-par movies.

"But," said McAllister, "this was for the boss and the boss gets to work however he wants."

In one respect, though, *Willow* dazzled audiences. ILM showcased an entirely new computer animation technique it had devised—morphing. Scott Ross, whom Lucas had recruited the year of *Willow*'s debut as director of operations for strategic planning and new technologies, strongly urged Lucasfilm patent and market the software. Lucas never got around to it. "He still slaps his forehead talking about the morph phenomenon," Ross said in 2001. "ILM missed the market opportunity, and now someone else's morphing program sells off-the-shelf for $95."

Meanwhile, under Ross's guidance, ILM tripled in size and regained its leadership in state-of-the-art special effects production. *Who Framed Roger Rabbit?, The Abyss*, and *Indiana Jones and the Last Crusade* all bore ILM's imprint. Ross attempted to persuade Lucas that ILM should not only be servicing other people's movies but creating original ones in-house as well—which would mean encouraging more creative minds at Skywalker Ranch. But amazingly, sources say, Ross was only able to meet personally with Lucas half-a-dozen times, and Lucas apparently stuck to his guns that there was room for only one filmmaker in his organization. Ross steered ILM into TV commercials, turning Lucasfilm Commercial Productions into the company's most profitable division. Impatient *Star Wars* fans accused Lucas of selling out and continued clamoring for another episode.

The success in 1989 of *Indiana Jones and the Last Crusade*—$100 million at the box office in only two weeks—spurred Lucas to embark on a new personal project: the George Lucas Educational Foundation. His companies would produce the TV series *Young Indiana Jones*, in which the main character would meet famous personalities in history—Lawrence of Arabia, Sigmund Freud, Pablo Picasso and Archduke Ferdinand of Austria. Participating schools would receive study guides, opportunities for interactive classroom sessions, turning the TV series, said Lucas's biographer John Baxter, into a "vehicle for turning American kids on to the wonders of history and the thrill of exploring the world." The *Young Indiana Jones* production crew filmed for 117 weeks, traveled to over 20 countries, and shot over 15,000 camera set-ups. Ten thousand schools signed up for the project.

But unfortunately, the series never caught on. There were two practical problems. First, Young Indiana Jones couldn't commit historical inaccuracies—preventing an assassination, for example—for the sake of drama. Second, real heroes of history didn't interact with the fictional Young Indy. They were doing the things that encyclopedias, biographies, and textbooks said they really were. So Young Indy became a bystander watching from the sidelines.

By 1991, ILM had become a kind of factory for special effects in other company's movies, many of them with mediocre plots. Said ILM's John Lassetter, who would later direct *Toy Story* for Pixar, "You'd kill yourself on effects, but no one remembered the films." Scott Ross quit to start his own company. In the Lucasfilm's company history, his name is mentioned only once, as if to say his contribution was unimportant. Company president Doug Norby and a number of other executives quit in 1992.

That year, The Academy of Motion Picture Arts and Sciences honored Lucas with the Irving Thalberg Award, given to a "creative producer whose body of work reflects a consistently high quality of motion picture production." Steven Spielberg presented the Thalberg statue to George at the Academy Awards Ceremony.

But in fact, Lucas was temporarily at a creative and financial dead-end. He was living in seclusion at Sky-walker Ranch (several years earlier, fellow Californian president Ronald Reagan had requested a tour of the ranch. Lucas, angry that he had been legally unable to

Steven Spielberg presenting the Irving Thalberg Award to Lucas on behalf of the Academy of Motion Picture Arts and Sciences. Despite receiving the award, Lucas himself was at a stagnant point in his career in 1992.

prevent Reagan from referring to his Strategic Missile Defensive Initiative in speeches as "Star Wars," refused a visit.) As a director, he had not been in the chair since 1976. Movie rights to his early films were eroding from a legal point of view, yet he continued to hoard control over his companies and their finances. With the exodus of Ross, Norby, and other executives, it seemed likely the fiercely independent filmmaker who had proudly spurned Hollywood might become like the main character in

Orson Welles' movie *Citizen Kane*—a remote, imperious has-been. In 1994, *Radioland Murders*, adapted from a script he'd penned years earlier, flopped in theaters. Symbolically, as if entering an artifact in its collection, the Library of Congress honored *American Graffiti* in 1995 as one of the 25 named to the National Film Registry.

But technology may again have rescued Lucas from a permanent fade-out on the filmmaking scene. By the mid-1990s, advances in digital technology—in sound, editing, and special effects—had reached a point where many of the burdens of filmmaking that Lucas disliked so much had evaporated. In the quiet of a high-tech studio, digital techniques enable directors to manipulate actors, scenery, and lighting, reducing the need for extended filming on location, or for coaching performances from real people. The only service performed by actors for 2001's life-like *Monster's Inc.*, for example, was providing voice-overs. (Disney even added "out-takes" and "bloopers," as if the animated characters were live actors who muffed their lines or tripped while walking.) Said Lucas, "Digital technology is the same revolution as adding sound to pictures and the same revolution as adding color to pictures." And it would free him at last from the kinds of dreadful personal experiences he suffered directing the first *Star Wars* episode in Tunisia.

So when in 1997, Carrie Fisher—who played Princess Leia from the trilogy—presented an actor costumed as Chewbacca with the Lifetime Achievement Award at the MTV Awards in June, it was as if closing the door on that kind of filmmaking. That year, *Star Wars: Episode I: The Phantom Menace* went into production.

In 1998, 20th Century Fox distributed a remastered trilogy to theaters across North America in preparation for the release of the new episode. Lucasfilm released the *Star*

Lucas with some of the original cast at the premiere of *Star Wars Special Edition* in 1997. The release coincided with the original trilogy being released in theaters, building up to the release of *Episode 1: The Phantom Menace*.

Wars Special Edition collection for fans who wanted an updated version of the series. As the century drew to a close, the American Film Institute's list of America's 100 greatest movies included *Star Wars*, *Raiders of the Lost Ark*, and *American Graffiti*.

In the spring of 1999, 30,000 *Star Wars* fans gathered in Denver, Colorado for a three-day Star Wars Celebration sponsored by the Official Fan Club. At the same time, eager fans lined up at theaters across the country to see *The Phantom Menace*. In a way, *The Phantom Menace* was a bridge from the past to the future. Not only was it the first episode in the prequel series, and the resumption of the *Star Wars* saga, but it was one of the last of Lucas' movies to employ film.

Star Wars: Episode II: Attack of the Clones, released in 2002, is an all-pixel, "film free" production with real actors. "For the cast," said Lucas, "it didn't make much difference except that they didn't get interrupted as often. You don't want a lot of time between takes; if you have to stop to reload the camera, it has a tendency to dissipate a lot of the energy that an actor's developing to get the performance right. [For the crew] the biggest issue was that we could see dailies while we were shooting."

As the *Star Wars* series draws to close by 2005, Lucas imagines that more and more theaters will be using digital projectors, and THX sound equipment. "But there's no way that we're going to threaten the movie theaters," says Lucas. "That would be suicidal."

From the Skywalker Ranch—a compound of quaint Victorian buildings on 4,700 acres—into which Lucas ultimately poured $200 million, he directs the activities of his companies, newly rejuvenated by the digital revolution he is helping to create. The property includes stables, a softball diamond, three restaurants, a vineyard and its own fire department.

The multi-award-winning Lucas group of companies also includes LucasArts, which develops and publishes interactive entertainment software; Lucas Digital, made up of Industrial Light & Magic and Skywalker Sound, which creates visual effects and audio post-production for the entertainment industry; Lucas Licensing, which handles merchandising for all of Lucasfilm's film and television properties; and Lucas Learning, which offers interactive educational software.

The Ranch isn't visible from the nearest road. After reaching the offices of ILM, visitors must drive into the countryside of Marin County about 15 to 20 minutes, crossing several small streams. No photographs are allowed.

The ranch house is a beautiful building of Victorian design, framed by green hills and a small lake. The entrance hall features a grand staircase on the right, which winds majestically left as it rises to the second floor, and Lucas' private office. Lucas had the hand-assembled redwood staircase re-done three times before he was satisfied with it. The interior redwood beams and supports of the entranceway were salvaged from old trestles and bridges under reconstruction. Nearby is the breakfast room, located to the left of the entrance hall, decorated in Colonial Williamsburg style and furnished with antiques. Adjoining the breakfast area is a reception room paneled in rich redwood, with soaring cathedral ceilings framed with beams milled on the ranch.

Down a hallway is the Skywalker Ranch library with isles of bookcases, thousands of books, and tables and chairs for the library's users. Research for sets, costumes, and historical figures—among many other things—takes place here. A 40-foot stained glass dome in the ceiling casts down sunlit colors of gold, red, and orange. A spiral staircase rises to a second floor, which holds more books and original paintings on the walls.

To the rear of the ranch house is a Victorian-style solarium. The three glass walls and a ceiling provide a panoramic a view of the ranch property, uncluttered by cars (concealed in underground garages). Inside the solarium, 30-foot trees rise from a lower level and pass through the center of the floor. In the basement is Lucas's private screening room. The room, approximately 25' wide by 50' long has 15 recliners, each accompanied by a marble end table with a touch-sensitive bankers lamp. The walls are draped with burgundy fabric for optimal listening to THX-produced sound.

Today, recently completed guest cottages named for famous figures in film—directors Orson Welles, John Huston, and Sergei Eisenstein, for example—have added to the ranch's mystique as a self-sufficient community of writers, designers, graphic artists, and actors far from Hollywood. Currently, construction is underway for relocating ILM, LucasArts, Lucas Learning Ltd., Lucas Online, and the George Lucas Educational Foundation to the Presidio, a former military base in San Francisco. Although Lucas has run into some objections from the city council regarding his plans, he intends to build a $250 million, 1,500-employee corporate campus, a high-tech Presidio museum, and a seven-acre "Great Lawn" that will be open to the public.

To the ranch will be added 109,000 square-feet of office space, a 60,000 square-foot archives building, a maintenance facility, gatehouse, digital film production facility, day-care center, a lodge for meetings, and a gym.

The Phantom Menace was the last of Lucas' movies to use film. The next installment in the saga, *Attack of the Clones*, will be fully digital in production.

Chapter 8

The Future of Filmmaking

I think I've made some changes in the way the film industry works, and I think there will be more dramatic changes to come. I'm enthusiastic about that and I have a feeling that will be part of my legacy.

—George Lucas

TO GEORGE LUCAS, the future of filmmaking is digital.

"I think crossing into the digital age is the big move for the industry," he told the American Academy of Achievement.

"I think it will be the biggest thing that's happened while I've been making movies . . . I don't see any other major technical process coming along and changing that." Other directors will be slow to come around to the new technology, he expects. But that doesn't change what he believes is the inevitability of digital production in moviemaking. "They're just very cautious; they'll get around to it in time," he said in an interview with *Time* magazine. "It's happening whether anybody likes it or not. I have some friends, like Marty [Scorsese] and Steven [Spielberg], and they're not going to change over. They love film. I think Jim Cameron and Francis [Ford Coppola] changed over. It's like the beginning of color. Some people still wanted to use black and white, and that's great. It's an addition to what's already existing."

Greater use of digital production makes sense to Lucas for several reasons. First, it gives freer rein to artistic expression. Landscapes that have never been seen before, ancient marching armies, and legions of mythological creatures can be created (or recreated) electronically. "So now you can tell much more interesting stories and you can express yourself more clearly," says Lucas. "That's what's happening today, and that's why all artists are constantly pushing the technology, the medium—to widen the range, so that they can use their imagination." Lucas believes that although digital production permits the creation of photo-realistic human beings, live actors will never be completely eliminated from filmmaking. On the other hand, the ability to digitally create much more realistic aliens is what encouraged him to resume the *Star Wars* saga. Referring to the creatures in *The Phantom Menace*, Lucas said, "I've gotten much better performances out of my aliens this time."

Second, digital production has a practical side that appeals to any cost-conscious filmmaker. Casts needn't wait as long as they once did for film to be reloaded—inserting a new chip or switching to another drive is a major asset in an industry where time is literally money. And for the director and crew, digital permits reviewing every scene mere seconds after it's completed. This means no more waiting until evening when the "dailies," as they're called, have been developed, printed, and are available for viewing.

But Lucas also points out the moviemaking is becoming no longer the exclusive territory it once was. At one time, Hollywood had the film industry in a hammerlock—still does, in the minds of many small independent filmmakers. "But that too is changing, says Lucas, "and again, the digital revolution is behind it. I think there are going to be some social changes that take place due to the Internet, and the availability of the tools to more and more people. I think you are going to find a lot of people recutting movies and changing them, making them into their own movies, things that are hard to contemplate at this point. And there will be delivery systems that are way, way different."

In other words, there will be more competition from self-made moviemakers who are using an inexpensive technology to get the public's attention. Directors who insist on using film exclusively may be driving themselves to extinction. The "way, way different" delivery systems Lucas describes have to do with the getting movies into theaters, which is where they make their money—and there too, digital has the advantage. "I think the biggest issue is going to be to be how the movies get into the marketplace and what happens to them once they are there," says Lucas. "I don't think it's going to be a 'sit down, hands off' situation anymore. I think it's going to be people sort of reinventing the movies once they're out there. How this works for the artist, I don't know. And what it does to the marketplace, I don't know. We're living in very exciting times and I look forward to seeing how this whole thing evolves."

Lucas looks forward to democratization of moviemaking through the aid of digital production. As an example, in the past, ILM has charged $25 million per film for special effects. But for the film *The American President*, the entire House of Representatives was recreated—complete with an digitalized audience of listeners—for much less than what it would have cost to rent the actual House of Representatives and populate it with thousands of extras. Lucas hopes that someday two filmmakers in a garage will be able use digital video technology to make their feature-length movie for just few thousand dollars.

He denies that that the excitement he feels about digital production is just his love of technology affecting his judgment. To Lucas, the new methods hold greater potential to tell a better story. "I know I have a reputation for being this technical guy, but I'm not. All I know is I need to tell a story, and I'm most interested in quality . . . so the audience can enjoy the film the same way we do when we sit in the answer print screening and see it under the most prime conditions. The idea in digital projection is that you get a high quality image for the run of the film."

Although it raises the hackles of directors, screenwriters, critics—and perhaps audiences as well—Lucas prefers to think of the heart of filmmaking as technical. "The craft of movies is almost completely technical," Lucas argues, "as opposed to writing a book or something, which is only partially technical . . . whether we add sound, or whether we add color, or whether we use digital technology, is

Lucas sees the future of filmmaking as being a totally digital affair—not only because of his love of technological advancements, but because of his need for control and independence as a filmmaker.

simply a way of broadening the canvas, so that we have more colors to work with."

It's not much a stretch to conclude then that Lucas also sees digital production as a means to maintain his independence. The man who bristled when a big studio recut his first feature, *THX-1138*, who built his studios far from Hollywood, who waited 20 years between directing films, no doubt sees more in-house, creative control over his movies as yet another benefit of digital production. Speaking of his need to remain out from under the thumbs of others, Lucas said:

> For me it's very important. Most creative people don't like others looking over their shoulder saying, 'Why don't you make that green? Why don't you make that blue? Why are you doing this?' . . . . So you try to get yourself into a situation where you only have to answer to yourself, where you can ask advice of people, and work with your peers and mentors to do the best job you can possibly do. There's nothing worse than the frustration of having somebody who doesn't get what you're doing trying to turn it into something else. It's a very frustrating thing and I never wanted to go through it . . . . That attitude comes out of film school, I think, where the primacy of the creative process in making a film is what you live for. It's not a business. It's trying to create something interesting that you're proud of, and try out creative ideas that may seem really off the wall, may work or may not work.

And he admits that many times his creations don't work, which is a trade-off of assuming the risk of success or failure all oneself. "Sometimes people are surprised to learn that most of the films I've made don't work," says Lucas. "They've been released but nobody has ever seen them. Maybe 40 percent of them are very successful. When my films that don't work it's usually because I tried some very experimental idea. I tried new ideas and they just didn't work, as opposed to trying to do something conventional and having it be so conventional nobody wanted to see it."

It can be argued, of course, that Lucas's riches—from countless merchandising deals, production facilities valued at half a billion dollars, and rights to some of the most successful films of the 20th century—gives him the luxury of being easy about success or failure. But Lucas is the first to say that money should be neither the motivation nor the reward if someone is thinking of going into the film business. "I want to tell film students: 'If you've gone into films to make money, fame and fortune, just forget it! The odds are way against you. Go into the stock market! Go into something else. You're never going to find money in the film business. Because it's too hard' . . . I've got just about as much money as you can get, and I was just as happy 30 years ago. As long as I could make a movie, I was happy. And as long as I still can make movies, I'll still be happy."

Looking ahead to the future of his career, Lucas says his main concern now is that time is closing in. "[F]or me it's just a matter of 'How can I get through all the stories in the amount of time I have left?' My dream is that I get to do it. That was my dream when I was younger, too. 'Will I get to make the movies? Will I get to do what I want?'"

If his past is any prediction of his future, he will continue to rely on his instincts—about what he wants to do, how to do it, and what people enjoy. "I've always just followed my own course," says Lucas, "whatever I found the most

Lucas feels pride in being one of the innovators and advocates of new technology in filmmaking. He has already used digital technology to create characters and entire armies of extras in *The Phantom Menace*. Mark Hamill had remarked in the past, "I have a sneaking suspicion that if there were a way to make movies without actors, George would do it."

interesting to me at the moment. I've never had a real plan of, 'I want to get from here to there, and I've got to do this.' The underlying plan to everything is, 'I've got a bunch of movies to tell, and this is the one I'm going to do now, and this is the one I'm going to do next.' And then I focus on the one at hand."

Looking back over his career, Lucas is proud that he "helped move cinema from a chemical-based medium to a digital-based medium." He's also left a body a work if others to study and examine—a collection of stories, as he prefers to call them—but which works in his legacy will be appreciated in the future is a mystery that he doesn't want to contemplate. As he says, "You may make something you don't think is very important during your lifetime and it'll last for a thousand years. You can't really focus too much on that part of it, because you don't know what history is going to throw at you in terms of what's important and what's not important."

But he remains confident that he has made "changes in the way the film industry works," he says, "and I think there will be more dramatic changes to come. I'm enthusiastic about that and I have a feeling that will be part of my legacy."

1944 George Walton Lucas Jr. born in Modesto, California on May 14

1962 Hospitalized three days before high school graduation as a result of a serious auto accident while drag racing

1964 Graduates from Modesto Junior College, Modesto, CA with a two-year Associate of Arts (AA) degree

1966 Makes several short films as a student at University of Southern California. *Electronic Labyrinth: THX-1138: 4EB,* takes first prize at the 1967-68 National Student Film Festival; graduates from University of Southern California with a Bachelor of Fine Arts (BFA) degree

1967 Awarded a scholarship by Warner Brothers to observe the filming of *Finian's Rainbow,* directed by Francis Ford Coppola

1969 Founds American Zoetrope independent production company with Coppola. Begins production of *THX-1138*; marries Marcia Lucas (née Griffin), film editor, February 22

1971 Incorporates Lucasfilm Ltd.; releases *THX-1138*, released on March 11 as an American Zoetrope Production

1973 Releases *American Graffiti* August 2, which receives five Academy Award nominations, and the Golden Globe, the New York Film Critics' and National Society of Film Critics' awards

1974 Begins writing *Star Wars* and working on preliminary set designs

1975 Establishes Industrial Light & Magic to produce the visual effects for *Star Wars*, and Sprocket Systems (later Skywalker Sound) to edit and mix the movie

1977 Releases *Star Wars* on May 25, which becomes the largest grossing film to that date, and receives six Academy Awards for original score, film editing, sound, art and set decoration, costume design and visual effects, as well as Special Achievement Academy Award for sound effects creations

1980 Releases *The Empire Strikes Back* May 21, which breaks opening day records, and receives an Academy Award for best sound and a Special Achievement Academy Award for visual effects; begins construction on Skywalker Ranch

1981 Releases *Raiders of the Lost Ark* June 21, which receives Academy Awards for art direction, sound, film editing and visual effects, as well as a Special Achievement Academy Award for sound-effects editing

1983 Releases *Return of the Jedi* May 25, which breaks opening day records and receives a Special Achievement Academy Award for visual effects along with five Academy Award nominations; divorces Marcia Lucas

1984 Releases *Indiana Jones and the Temple of Doom* May 23, which receives an Academy Award for visual effects

1986 Executive produces *Captain Eo* for Disneyland and Walt Disney World, directed by Francis Coppola and starring Michael Jackson; sells Pixar to Steven Jobs; co-produces *Labyrinth* with Henson Associates

1988 Releases *Willow* on May 20, which receives two Academy Award nominations, and *Tucker: The Man and His Dream* on August 12, which receives four Academy Award nominations

1989 Releases *Indiana Jones and the Last Crusade* on May 24, which receives an Academy Award for sound-effects editing; establishes LucasArts Entertainment Company, which includes the Games Division

1992 Honored by The Academy of Motion Picture Arts and Sciences with the Irving Thalberg Award, given to a "creative producer whose body of work reflects a consistently high quality of motion picture production"

1997 Releases The *Star Wars Special Edition* on January 31; *The Empire Strikes Back Special Edition* premieres February 21; The *Return of the Jedi Special Edition* premieres March 14

1999 Releases *The Phantom Menace*, following charity premieres that raise $5.6 million, on May 19, becoming at that time the second-highest worldwide grossing film ever released

2002 Releases *Attack of the Clones*, the fifth Star Wars movie

1969 *The Rain People*

1971 *THX-1138*

1973 *American Graffiti*

1977 *Star Wars*

1980 *The Empire Strikes Back*

1980 *Kagemusha*

1981 *Body Heat*

1981 *Raiders of the Lost Ark*

1983 *Twice Upon a Time*

1983 *Return of the Jedi*

1984 *Indiana Jones and the Temple of Doom*

1984 *The Ewok Adventure* (TV)

1985 *Ewoks: The Battle for Endor* (TV)

1985 "Ewoks" (TV Series)

1985 "Droids" (TV Series)

1986 *Labyrinth*

1986 *Captain Eo*

1986 *Howard the Duck*

1987 *Star Tours*

1988 *Tucker: The Man and His Dream*

1988 *The Land Before Time*

1988 *Willow*

1989 *Indiana Jones and the Last Crusade*

1989 "The Young Indiana Jones Chronicles" (TV Series)

1994   *Radioland Murders*

1994–99   *Adventures of Young Indiana Jones Series*

1999   *Star Wars: Episode I—The Phantom Menace*

2002   *Star Wars: Episode II—Attack of the Clones*

Baxter, John. *Mythmaker: The Life and Work of George Lucas*. New York: Avon/Spike, 1999.

Brosnan, John. *The Primal Screen*. London: Orbit, 1991.

Champlin, Charles. *George Lucas: The Creative Impulse*. New York: Harry N. Abrams, Inc., 1992.

Goldberg, Lee, et al. *Science Fiction Filmmaking in the 1980s*. Jefferson, NC: McFarland, 1995.

Henderson, Mary. *Star Wars: The Magic of Myth*. New York: Bantam, 1997.

Jenkins, Garry. *Empire Building: The Remarkable Real Life Story of Star Wars*. 1997. Secaucus, NJ: Carol Publishing, 1999.

Pollock, Dale. *Skywalking: The Life and Films of George Lucas*. New York: Harmony, 1983.

Salewicz, Chris. *George Lucas: The Making of His Movies*. New York: Thunder's Mouth Press, 1998.

White, Dana. *George Lucas*. (A & E Biography) Minneapolis, MN: First Avenue Editions, 1999.

Woog, Andrew. *George Lucas*. San Diego, CA: Lucent Books, 2000.

George Lucas: Entertainment Executive. The Hall of Business.
    The American Academy of Achievement.
    [www.achievement.org/autodoc/page/luc0pro-1]

Industrial Light & Magic (A Division of Lucas Digital Ltd.)
    [www.ilm.com/]

Skywalker Sound.
    [www.skysound.com/site.html]

Star Wars (the official site).
    [www.starwars.com/]

The Facts: George Lucas. E! Online Fact Sheet.
    [www.eonline.com/Facts/People/Bio/0,128,41002,00.html]

Charles J. Shields is the author of 12 books for Chelsea House. Before turning to writing fulltime, he was chairman of the English department at Homewood-Flossmoor High School in Flossmoor, Illinois. His 1985 book, *The College Guide for Parents* (The College Board) won an award from the Educational Press Association. He has degrees in English and history from the University of Illinois, Urbana-Champaign. Shields lives in Homewood, Illinois with his wife, Guadalupe, an educational consultant in reading and literacy to the Chicago Public Schools.